Self Genesis:
For the Emancipated Minds Only!

A Knowledge of Self Handbook

BY CHISTRO DERTEASE

Copyright © 2018 CRAZYCHI DESIGNS PRESS CORP.

All rights reserved.

ISBN:1732581703
ISBN-13: 978-1732581708

Dedication Message

I dedicate this Book to my Ancestors for laying the Foundation for me to be Here and to the Divine Order for the Honor and Privilege to Serve as a Light for my People. This is for the loving memory of my grandmother, Neille Linder for being my first master teacher for the Guidance, the exposure to Cultural Arts and Discipline.

Special shout out to my Loving FAM, my wonder daughter, Jasz and real Friends for showing love, always having my back THROUGH Trust. Loyalty. Teamwork. To my home, the city of Chicago for being survivor; destined for a true Awakening, Healing and Community Cooperation. For the Tribe Worldwide for a Future One Unity Community! To my Fellow LightWorkers and the many Beautiful Muses of the Light for making Positive changes a Reality and inspiring Good Vibes. To the Youth of the World who need the Self-Knowledge and will take these Principles to Higher Levels that I could only Dream of.

And to YOU the Reader of this Handbook...Thank You for being of Open Mind, Heart, and Spirit. Ase'

Striving for Love, Order, Peace, Positive Vibes and Greatness,

Chistro Dertease

Aka CrazyCHI

"The Meastro from Chicago"

For Free Inspiration follow my IG @therealcrazychi

Preamble

I am who you are. I am a visionary who is directly speaking to a fellow visionary. We are connected through the light, and we are living in an age in which darkness has distorted that light. Although there are many forms of spiritual practices and self-help tools available, **Self Genesis** aims to awaken and enlighten you to your higher self! As an overcomer from PTSD, anxiety disorder, clinical depression, child abuse, and self-destructive behaviors I can attest that the information in this spiritual manifesto has not only helped me heal but also reconnect my spirituality and elevated me higher than I ever did within a religious practice. I trust that I have achieved the Messiah, Christ or Messianic spiritual level, which you are more than capable of reaching and surpassing if you allow yourself to be open and engaged in the process.

Knowledge of Self requires time and consistency!

Self-knowledge is essential to self-love so, practice the art of unconditional love!

This information is meant to enlighten, inspire, engage, and reimagine our sense of purpose while utilizing life-applied principles with love and understanding! There is enough inside of you to unlock the matrix, so use it! Our imagination is our inner superpower and we must cultivate it.

The youth are unlocked before they get here so remember to feed their curiosity with a solid foundation of self-expression, knowledge of self, unconditional love, and the freedom to be creative! I call upon our youth to become self-aware and young masters of thyself, and that adults model self-mastery principles by leading by example.

There are too many labels, too many truths mixed with lies, and too many confused souls desperately searching for simple truths that they can just activate within themselves; when lost. We all should have a moral compass ready because we are all capable of getting lost at any time. But we must use the self-mastery tools that were made for us, as individuals and as a collective. These tools require you to know how to use them. So learning about yourself will make you better equipped to use the Divine given tools inside you.

Let's understand that we have a higher self as well as a lower self. To deny any existence of the self is to deny Self. Being honest means being the real you! Who are you, when the world is asleep, and you are the only one up? Staring directly at yourself in the mirror, you should know better than anyone who you really are from the inside out. This reflection doesn't just refer to your light or higher self, but your shadow or lower self. As multi-dimensional beings we carry the ability to be the victim, villain and vanguard in this life. Which role do you carry? Can you say out loud what you stand for or why you get up every day and do what you do? What drives you? What is your Divine purpose in this lifeline? Where do you want to go?

We must often reflect, ask and question ourselves as we may oftentimes get sidetracked and forget the why and the where. Knowledge of Self, if practiced with an open mind and a sincere heart and using this **Self Genesis** handbook, will help you discover dynamic layers beyond your current existence and overstanding of Self. Do you take chances for fun or growth? Do you value spiritual development as well as physical? Now is the time to take the challenge of spiritual growth seriously with genuine intentions!

I pledge that this material is authentically inspired from my personal spiritual training with the Divine Order, and it will contain personal exposures from various religions, positive affirmations, astrology, numerology, and other forms of spiritual practices. The purpose is to provide the seeker of spiritual growth a safe, open minded, nonjudgmental Self-guide, void of any hero worship, religious dogma or fear-based indoctrination. **Self Genesis** will empower you to achieve your most fabulous self through applied knowledge, self-discovery, unconditional love, and positive vibes. Simplifying the matrix to a basic level to make it readily available for all to understand! The main themes are Awareness, Knowledge of Self, Self Love, and Selfless Service.

I only ask that you pledge to keep your faith in YOU (no matter your religious affiliation or spiritual practices), be open-minded (you must be aware of what you know and what you may not know). And be consistent with yourself; go at the speed that you can truly commit to without excuses! Apply what you need at the moment and work through the steps. Lastly, love yourself and be patient with whatever part of the Self you are working on. This is not just about spiritual growth but becoming a holistic, world-saving heroes/anti-heroes for our world, which many already are; ways to get involved will be covered last in 'Ways to Launch the Age of Aquarius'! I am happy and honored to share, be prepared to have some fun! Thank you for your presence and have a wonderful journey to your GREATER Self. Ase'

Positive vibes only!

Table of Contents

Dedication Message 1
Preamble 3
Table of Contents 8
Introduction 9
Disclaimer 11
Chapter 1: The Process 12
Chapter 2: Awareness 16
Chapter 3: Knowledge of Self 26
Chapter 4: Self Love 40
Chapter 5: Selfless Service 54
Chapter 6: Ways to Launch Age of Aquarius 58

Introduction

Self Genesis: A Knowledge of Self Handbook will be taught at a fundamental level on up from a first-hand account. Know that religion and spirituality are two entirely separate things. Numerology can be your best friend. The homework challenges provided is optional, but for spiritual growth, it is mandatory!

The Divine Sends Us Messengers to keep us updated on the divine course, so please enjoy with an open mindset, and be ready to learn. Positive vibes can manifest for you quicker if you read while listening to transient music or calming, soothing instrumentals in a safe space.

We also can raise our frequencies using empowering words that create a new era of expectations that require the Self to elevate. Throughout this handbook, you will recognize new spellings from old, outdated words. The definitions are provided for clarification.

Key Definitions

*The Divine Order- The trust, belief or faith in a higher power, one source, one connection, one truth, and in accordance with the universal laws.

*Ase'- Declaration to speak or manifest truth; closing in divine prayer or speech. Acknowledge. Speak. Exist!

*Huemyn- a wise, compassionate, principled, and soulful being. A cosmic being existing on the plane of Earth.

*Positive vibes- a state of being, living in the now with good intentions; creating good energy that allows you to be open-minded, transparent, giving, and receiving to yourself and others!

*Visionaries- A positive change agent, one who sees the forest beyond the trees, serving as a catalyst for social transformation; often referred to as lightworkers.

*Safe space- a comfortable, peaceful, relaxing area, place, or spot in which you can relax, chill, and focused on receiving new information.

*Anti-huemynism- any policy or practice that exploits, harms, or devalues huemyn beings and/or their living environment.

Disclaimer

I will move forward under the affirmation of a Divine Order and the New Golden Rule, which will be covered later in the material. Following the natural flow of the Divine Order will allows us to build, love and live in goodwill. We don't have to be alike or share the same belief systems, but we must have at least a basic level of mutual respect for each other. Coexistence works when we make the conscious effort to cultivate on peaceful terms. We get to peaceful terms by creating and sharing peaceful morals and values that we actively practice!

The Moral and Value Systems you create for yourself is a personal decision!

The acceptance and appreciation of thySelf comes by consciously developing your own moral and value system, which should evolve your sense of connection, wholeness, and empathy! Self-knowledge is a daily practice, so don't get lazy and don't limit the warm-ups!

It took me nine years of spiritual practice to improve my spiritual growth to where I am now. So, slow and steady truly wins the race!

    Just trust the process!

Chapter 1: The Process

The process can be intimidating, long, tedious, but also spiritually rewarding! Be in the NOW of this part of your journey & NOT fixated on the destination!

<u>Things to Remember</u>

You are a Visionary! Creation of a safe space is inside you. The information contained in this material will help you develop your vision for your self-space.

Pace and patience are key!

Be of Positive Vibes- an open mind, heart, spirit, and of good intentions to unlock your most magnificent self and quite possibly your divine spiritual level.

You will recognize 'Positive Vibes Only' throughout the teachings. They serve as a friendly reminder to be in alignment with your positive, open mindset to fully benefit from the information.

Trust the Process to Create a New System.

Purpose

To provide the seeker of spiritual growth a safe, nonjudgmental Self-guide, void of any hero worship or negative intentions to achieve the greatest self through applied knowledge, Self-discovery, unconditional love, and positive vibes.

By learning and sharing ways to improve spiritual level, detox from outdated systems, and master thyself.

Goal

To provide a basic, simplistic foundation for anyone on any (social, academic, spiritual, age, etc.) level to process the Knowledge of Self-concepts into their everyday lives.

Since Knowledge of Self is Power, then Knowledge of Self is Absolute Power! Everyone should take the opportunity to know and build thyself, and learning how is part of that process.

Self Themes

Awareness 1, 2 & 3- The Beginning of Discovery

Knowledge of Self 1, 2 & 3- Who are You? Knowledge of Self is the Most Important Knowledge in the World!

Self-Love 1, 2 & 3- Unconditional Love of Self Attracts and Radiates, Unconditionally.

Selfless Service- Act of the Divine is through Our Works

<u>Added Concept for Application</u>

Ways to Launch Age of Aquarius- We Can Create an Empowering, System when We are Ready!

<u>Self-work (H.W.) Challenge</u>

Self-work is needed to ensure that you manage to apply the information not just reading it!

I yearn for every one of you to reach that next level of Self, whether It's the Messiah (Messenger) level or not. As long as you get your spiritual gains, then you are winning! We have to be ready to change Not Just Talk About it, So H.W. is Essential!

At the End of the Day,

You must be willing to do the:

Self- Heart Work, Self- Heal Work, and Self- Health Work

Trust the Process. Every Theme has Self Work, so embrace it!

Warm Ups

Throughout the handbook are what I like to refer to as 'mental stretch warm ups' to ensure that you are in the now when reading the information and are open. The Warm Ups are at the beginning of each chapter for mental and spiritual clarity, and to physically align ourselves to the here and now; to fully engage in the process of self-development and self-discovery!

Chapter 2: Awareness

We are focusing now from an awareness standpoint to the Divine Order.

If you are religious, this handbook recognizes the existence of a Divine Order.

If you are spiritual, it will provide the basics to advance approach on frequency levels.

If you are advanced, use this handbook to stay grounded, review, or share the access to the light!

We are ALL at different spiritual levels, which are all right on, but we must all come with an open heart to elevate!

We will now be entering the matrix.

Warm Ups!

In the beginning, there was nothingness, find a safe space and clear your mind for uninterrupted **3** minutes!

Now imagine you were sent to planet Earth void of any books or preconceived ideas on how life is on Earth, what is 5 things you would like to know before living life as a huemyn being?

Awareness

Awareness is defined as the knowledge or perception of a situation or fact. For the sake of the study, awareness is the basic level of understanding or consciousness.

Our first foundation to the knowledge of self is awareness. As babies, we are born into existence outside of our control. It is during this time we utilize our innate abilities, which can take over.

Our innate abilities are where we first use awareness!

So why is awareness so important?

Well, let's continue to examine what awareness does for the baby for a moment.

Babies babble to communicate, cry for attention or any form of nurturing, utilize natural reflexes to grasp, cry to be changed, and of course, cry for food. Babies display innate abilities not learned of this world, but divinely given!

For the next 10 minutes, explore and jot down at least 5 things babies do responsively, naturally.

So, what makes awareness important?

It's our innate connection to the natural order, which even without knowledge or information, the Divine sparks light inside each of us!

We are born spiritual beings above all else, the physical is just a vessel! YOU are born with specific presets, with an autonomous connection to the Divine Order without any outside interferences!

We are preset to react and respond as spiritual beings just like the animals!

Awareness Recap

Awareness is a basic level of understanding or consciousness.

By observing babies, you witness the basic level of awareness not taught by you!

This proves awareness is preset into the Huemyn consciousness from birth.

A preset to the Divine Order, which makes you and I spiritual beings!

Awareness H.W.

Write down at least 10 things you do responsively or naturally without thinking. (It can be tricks, habits, or talents done effortlessly)

Please make an effort in the H.W. before moving to the next chapters!

Warm Ups!

Clear your mind in a safe space for 3 minutes

Now deeply breathe in the positive vibes into the diaphragm, hold for 7 seconds, and release the old energy for 7 seconds for 10 reps!

Awareness 2- Spiritual Beings/ Huemyn Beings

Awareness 2 of the same whole

Spiritual Being= spiritual self

Huemyn Being= physical self

Types of Spiritual Self Practices!

Included but not limited to religion, prayer, acts of kindness, earthly art conductors, unconditional love, meditation, food and drink, medicinal use, being in nature, and fasting.

As Spiritual Beings, we are designed with the need or longing to practice our spiritual selves! We reenergize through our connection to the natural order! Many portals can be used to reach the Divine Order!

Any religion or spiritual practice that justified or justifies using slavery or any forms of huemyn exploitation at any point is anti-huemyn and thus incapable of being of or from the Divine Order. We forgive and forget too quickly! No religion or spiritual practice can claim to be the sole path to spiritual growth and enlightenment! Be of the open spirit and not of a closed religion, take what may be helpful information and keep it moving.

Types of Physical Self Practices!

Included but not limited to exercising, playing outside, touching, art, all forms of physical fitness, sleeping, fasting, dietary lifestyle, meditation, medicinal use, writing, and other forms of creative self-expression.

As Physical Beings, we are designed to maintain the physical self in order to increase longevity!

Any practice that condones, justifies, or facilitates the mistreatment, abuses, or defiling of another for the sake of personal growth/development is, for all intents and purposes, void of the Divine Order! Huemyn exploitation is a terrible anti-huemyn behavior, not a divine one!

Self-practices help train the pillars and levels of the Self!

Spiritual Self	Mental Self	Emotional Self	Physical Self

The breakdown of Self has four pillars of the individual matrix of Self! A complex being interlocked between two realities: Physical & Spiritual realm! These realms can be altered at any time through emotional and mental factors, dietary lifestyle, environmental exposures, forms of programming, education, etc.!

Awareness comes into focus utilizing the basic from each pillar of Self!

Can you guess which pillar of Self is a baby touch On? All of the walls of Self are utilized! As we grow, we are to mature from Self-Awareness to Knowledge of Self!

We are Individual Matrixes within one cosmic, divine matrix known as the Universe!

Awareness 2 Recap

What we explored was the deeper level of our human awareness!

- Recognizing we are preset spiritual and physical beings.

- We use tools of self-practices to elevate Self.

- Our focused areas of self-awareness: emotional, mental, spiritual, and physical.

-No huemyn being was born to rule over another. No spiritual practice truly of the divine promotes or engages in human exploitation of any kind!

-All forms of self-practice should empower, not exploit, or harm self or others!

-We are matrixes within the Divine matrix!

Awareness 2 H.W.

Write down 2-5 ways you practice or activate each Self, daily!

Spiritual Self   Emotional Self

Mental Self   Physical Self

Warm Ups

Clear your mind for 3 minutes, then think of the first color that comes to mind. Name off: 10 Things known in that color!

Awareness 3 Additional Presets

Additional Presets/Preconditions Extend Beyond the Spiritual & Physical Beings that Also Help Play A Major Role in that First Awareness!

Parents
Birth Name
Born Day
Environment (Place of Birth)

Divine Number (Numerology)
Zodiac

Appearance

Characteristics, abilities, and talents are tied in some ways to our preconditions! For instance, my zodiac is Capricorn, born Jan. 2nd, with the divine number 9 which are a few examples of my additional presets! I can honestly say, learning more about my additional presets was vital in my spiritual awakening and a stronger sense of Self. Ase'

Take 10-15 minutes to map out a few of your additional presets!

Zodiac
Divine number
Birthday
Place of birth
Appearance

Each preset and conditions that exist at the time of birth of an individual immediately shapes a reality that develops a unique worldview from any other life form! Make sure to explore your divine spiritual number! By the way, numerology is not a religion.

Our Awareness helps the processing of information, which leads to know-how/ knowledge.

Therefore, self-awareness leads to self-knowledge!

Awareness 3 H.W.

Learn your divine number! Explore numerology and unlock another you!

Do your inner gifts match your divine number?

Before we start the new topic, I want to encourage everyone to practice the Self Work (H.W.) challenges! Wonderful work if you have done the H.W. challenges, if you can still do it. Please save the H.W. notes because they are for your future Self. So, take Self study with Pride!

The purpose of Awareness 1-3 was to: define awareness. Shed light on the huemyn preconditions. Explore the huemyn spiritual and physical duality. Understand the differences between spirituality and religion or any form of spiritual practice. Encourage new forms of positive self-practices.

Chapter 3: Knowledge of Self

Warm Ups

Clear your mind for 3 minutes

Then say your alphabets backward twice!

Based on what we have covered thus far,

What do you presume to be the most important question in the world?

From My Spiritual Studies, I have discovered that the meaning of life was an irrelevant question!

What does it value or improve the huemyn experience to know the meaning of life, when the answers to your very existence, your Divine purpose, are hidden within?

If the meaning of life for us is to sit in one space, would that prompt everyone to sit still? I think not. However, if it's revealed that your Divine purpose is to sit and create art, to share your positive vibes, and be of free mind, body, and spirit, you may consider this. For we, as spiritual beings need a sense of purpose and the Divine Order provides this for each one of us who become open-minded and self-aware. It was revealed to me that Knowledge of Self is the Most Important Knowledge in the world! Why?

Because without knowing who we are, we can't dare stand for something; and sure enough we become gullible to fall for anything! We must know our place on the board to properly play our best game. Ignorance is only blissful for the exploiter who knows. The only truth we can truly know, that will overcome ignorance in this lifetime, is the Self-truth! Truth is Divine, and Divine is the Truth! We can live divinely by living out our truth by being real in Self. Ase'

Knowledge of Self

The ability and process of learning and understanding one's Self-reflection through values, morals, personal disposition, likes, triggers, and unique characteristics! Learning how to convert self-awareness to self-knowledge!

Statement to Guide By

The Most Important Knowledge

is Knowledge of Self!

This is the statement that I Personally live by based on my spiritual practice with the Divine! No truth is most important than Self Truth! Like minds affirm each other. Thus, real recognizes real!

-Knowledge of Self is the most important knowledge because without knowing thySelf you are setting yourself up to fall for anything!

-You Must Be the PhD. of You!

-No One Can Think for You!

-The Divine judges on case-by-case basis, so you are responsible for your actions not anyone else!

The truth is hidden in each of us to unlock!

Self-denial is the enemy of the Self!

New Golden Rule

When you are faithful and committed to self-awareness, achieving knowledge of self, and become active in self-love through the practice of loving others, unconditionally, may you then unlock your divine spiritual level!

The New Golden Rule is A Foundation to Develop on Self, Morals, and Values in the Age of Aquarius! Ase'

Knowledge of Self Recap

-Knowledge of self is the process of converting self-awareness to self-know how.

-Knowledge of self is the most important knowledge in the world.

-The New Golden Rule is a guide to live by straight from the Divine Order! Please apply.

Knowledge of Self H.W.

Based on what you know you, summarize yourself in 2 sentences!

-Affirmation/Motivation-Positive vibes and open minds change the world!

Warm Ups

Clear your mind in a safe space for 2 minutes!

In addition, sitting or standing, side stretch to the left arching your right arm over your head (light pull from the left hand) hold for 15 or 30 seconds. Now reverse to the right side, left arm over the head (light pull from the right hand) for 15 or 30 seconds.

Knowledge of Self 2

Higher Self vs. Lower Self

Enclosed in each and everyone one of us is our lower and higher selves! The only differences that separate the two are the values and the moral systems we self-impose!

(Usually, by way of family, school, peers, societal constructs, and religious practices; social media, etc. are how we acquired our initial set of moral codes and values)

We hold an inner being which holds a lower and higher Self.

No one is totally oneself and no one is completely incapable of reaching higher ranges of Self. Knowing this observable information should keep you mindful of balance and humility.

Achievement of Higher self requires:

Morals foster an ethics system based on your outside perception of right and wrong, good and, bad, or helpful and harmful behavior.

Values are the principles you stand for personally. Heavily influenced by experiences and environment, they are likely to change often! Both morals and values create our code of conduct.

Morals and Values are the tools that guide us through this life. We can learn to live in peace with a universal commitment to learn, share, and love each other with great intentions.

Higher Self- Expressions of Unconditional love for self, others, and nature or performing selfless acts, good deeds, and standing up for the defenseless or exploited are prime examples of higher self-behavior. The high frequency Self.

Lower self- Acts of abuse, forms of exploitation or depreciation of huemyn life, self harm and mind manipulation are common examples of low self-behavior. The low frequency Self.

You must decide for yourself, what is the Lower Self and Higher Self within you? Design a realistic value & moral code of conduct that you can commit to following! Adhering to a set of values and ethics is needed even without a religious affiliation!

Morals and Values are what we use to properly guide us through this life experience. We can learn to live in peace with a universal commitment to live in peace and order. While also learning to love each other with great intentions.

For example, I began to have a spiritual breakthrough when I first learned the New Golden Rule! The enlightening dots connected, and my moral and value system changed! I no longer thought of myself separate from nature, but a part of the whole experience!

Therefore, I strongly value natural conservation, huemyn connections, planet sustainability, and the Divine Order! My Moral Code Stands that I Share My Spiritual Knowledge from the Divine freely with my fellow Visionaries, and love others unconditionally as I love my child! Ase'

If you are trying to achieve the higher Self, strive to live according to the Golden Rule given in the previous Knowledge of Self chapter!

The Art of Ying and Yang

Reminder to Maintain balance!

No one is one-way! Everything in moderation to stay grounded.

Balance yourself! Don't be so hard on yourself!

Everything should be done in moderation to avoid burning out and falling prey to deprived curiosity and thoughts.

Allow room to vent, make mistakes, learn lessons, and try new things that aren't Self-destructive!

Knowledge of Self 2 Recap

- Explained the differences between the higher Self and the lower Self

-Defined morals and values

-Stressed the Importance of having a moral and value system to elevate to higher Self

-Provided personal values and morals to give an example to clarify self-imposed moral and value system

-The importance of balance and moderation

Knowledge of Self 2 H.W.

Now it's time you exploring the self on a deeper level by creating your own programming code similar to a computer. What moral coding system do you have or want to cultivate for your life? And can you define it outside of religious texts? Answer the following challenges:

What is your faith system? What do you value? What is your moral compass?

Remember, a personal code of conduct is essential!

Warm Ups

Clear your mind for 5 minutes.

Name 5 new things you have learned about yourself thus far? What are you currently exploring about you?

Knowledge of Self 3-Self Map

Focusing on using self-imposed moral and value systems to create a personal life map!

The objective is to create an alternative matrix to explore yourself outside of indoctrination boundaries because the Divine Order is everywhere!

Self-Map Needs

In creating your life map, you can use your H.W. notes:

-Awareness H.W- Presets, natural abilities

-Knowledge of self H.W.

-Your Divine number

-2 sentences to summarize self

-Personal moral principles and values

We can assume that we know who we are until we are challenged to write it out! Which is why the Self work challenges were given to push you beyond the shallow understanding of you.

To be on your physical square is to be strong in self and in who you are. We mark our physical square by creating our Self map from the H.W. notes.

I will share my map from my notes as a visual:

I affirm my principles in sharing, sustainability, accountability, self-discovery, celebrating cultural identities.

I value trust, loyalty, and teamwork.

My moral compass is guided by the truth of self and faith in the Divine Order since we are One. I find being real and consistent with who you are, and this will help you grow spiritually. Thus, increasing your level of spirituality, and that there are no spiritual limits with possibility!

Things to Consider for your map:

Zodiac/Divine number
Abilities
Moral System

Values

Moral System

My Personal Self map for Example:

Zodiac/Divine number: Capricorn 9

Abilities: Unique problem solver, spiritually connected, a strong sense of justice, musically inclined.

Faith in a Divine Order that we are all connected and our higher self is the ideal state of being for peace of mind and positive vibes to exist.

My values: My divine connection, my child, family, peace of mind, huemynity, nature, youth development, empowerment, and Freewill.

My Personal Affirmation for Inspiration:

I fight, to live

I teach, to ensure the safety and prosperity of future lives!

I am a fighter, a liberator, a teacher!

My Triggers:

Positive- music production, creating positive affirmations, developing coping techniques, and teaching

Negative- selfish behavior, negativity dwellers, disloyalty and thieves.

I used researches on my zodiac and divine number to assist my in mapping out characteristics that I might have within.

I am convinced that our personal matrix has two squares. Physical square is based on your abilities and the things we stand on as truths about ourselves. And the Divine square is that role you were meant to be in accordance with the Divine Order. Each person has role in the world if we just explore deep within our dreams and imagination!

So next, I listed what my physical and divine squares are.

My physical square: writer/teacher, motivational speaker

Divine Square: spiritual messenger, lightworker

Lastly, I created my own personal mission statement to live by.

I am dedicated to sharing with all, especially the youth, spiritual information that will allow everybody to choose openly and honestly, who they wish to become. Supporting in the deconditioning of outdated information, reinforcing knowledge of self-normalizes self-responsibility and encourages positive vibes!

Knowledge of Self 3 H.W.

Use All Past H.W. Assignments to assist you!

-List your goal or likes

-The abilities that you have naturally

-Your physical square listing

- Write out your divine calling (if you know)

- Briefly list what inspires/triggers you: healthy and toxic!

-write one personal affirmation

-Write out a personal mission statement

If completed, how do you feel after creating your own Self map?

If you are still working in it, what you enjoying about the Self mapping process?

Knowledge of Self (1-3) Review

-Defined knowledge of self

-Provided the answer to the most important knowledge in the world

-Covered the New Golden Rule

-Explained the self-matrix: higher and lower self

-Touched on the Importance of balance like utilizing the art of Yin and Yang

-Designed our Self-map: Physical and Divine squares

Chapter 4: Self Love

Warm Up

Clear your mind in a safe space for 4 minutes!

Then, sit or stand and hug yourself for 2 minutes

Self-Love

Your sense of huemynity has love in it and self is where it is stored. So use it!

Self-love is the maintenance, treatment, and support of one's personal wellbeing.

Why should we have a love of self?

Self-love helps create a deep sense of value and appreciation of one's true self-worth.

What does self-love involve?

Wants vs. needs, pampering, triggers, healthy lifestyle, coping, personal conduct, self-aware vs. self-absorbed, holistic healing, freewill, protection, safe space, self behavior regulation, emotional intelligence, dwelling vs. reflecting, goals and aspirations, self-appreciation and appreciation of others, attention and affirmations, and forms artistic expression.

These are just some of the overwhelming number of areas of focus in regards to self-love

How are you in these areas? Take time to explore!

Self-love requires a balance of:

Emotional uplift, physical uplift, mental uplift, and spiritual uplift

The tools you use should be based on personal preference (here are a few examples)

Spa treatments. Any form of artistic expression. Accomplishing goals. Daily affirmations. Finding a sense of purpose. Health fitness. Detoxing and replenishing the body.

Without the balance of Self one could become:

Self-absorbed or self-deprecating

We must have the Self balance to prevent extremes. Utilizing the Art of Yin of Yang balance is key with manifesting positive vibes!

Self-love Goals

Learn to love yourself when no one is around.

Learn to love yourself when others are around.

Learn to love yourself in spite of other people's opinions of you.

Be vocal about how you would like to be treated, and be mindful of returning the same respect.

Real love doesn't need broadcasting. Therefore, demonstrate the love, don't brag!

A person of self-love doesn't render his or her self-respect!

Self-love Motivations

Self-love should strive to be unconditional.

Self-love is never selfish, but accepting and appreciative of Self.

Self-love is a process and shouldn't be overindulged, rushed nor should it be underutilized and neglected.

Self-love can shine your light or smother it, so be mindful!

Self Love H.W.

-lite assignment-

What's the one thing you love about you?

How does that love of you convey itself in your life?

Self-love is a reflection. Do you reflect light or darkness?

Last words

Self-love is the maintenance, treatment, and support of one's personal wellbeing.

Self-love helps create a broad sense of value and appreciation of one's true self-worth.

Self-love goals is a wonderful tool to use, add or create your own goals, as long as you stay balanced and mindful that you will be less likely to fall into extremes!

Self-love is vast and can't be fully covered in any reading material so don't limit yourself on positive resources.

We are almost done with the **Self Genesis** so let finish strong!

Warm Ups

Clear your mind in a safe space for 3 minutes!

Now search and listen to Nina Simone's "Aint got no, I got life" or any favorite empowerment of your own!

Then, speak of 3 things you are grateful for and 3 things you are hoping to achieve 3 months from now.

Inspiring and uplifting and is a wonderful Segway into Self-love installment!

Self-love 2 Digging Deeper

Awareness of Self through practice builds on knowledge of Self.

No one has to make sense of these things that make up you but you. And as long as the practices of Self is done in a healthy, constructive way! Which takes self-love and creates even more!

Remember.

You cannot equate your worth in money. The Divine created "incomprehensible" so we could never fully understand.

Destined to discover, make mistakes, fall, and fight to get back up!

However, we were also created to rival the work of no other inventor, which is why we were made "invaluable."

Destined to use our talents, imagination, and ingenuity to pursue life, liberty, and happiness.

Self-Love requires balance:

Emotional uplift is needed as we all have a fondness for feeling appreciated.

Spiritual uplift is needed as our connection, our internal battery, sense of being needs recharging often.

Physical uplift is needed as our vessels housing the spirit need good health to endure and protect.

Mental uplift is needed as the programming board; efficiency requires a daily nutritional equivalency and critical development.

<u>Self-love uplift</u>

We all have them.

Setbacks are bound to happen. No one can be 100% on point all the time, so don't be hard on yourself. Learn the lessons, make a sincere effort to grow yourself, love yourself, but own up to your mistakes, no excuses!

Self-harm and mistreatment is undeserved! Do not allow the unfortunate abuse of others to take you off your quest towards self-love.

<u>To enhance the flow of Positive Vibes</u>

Love Self-affirmations and friendly reminders are helpful simple tools, which is I encourage you to create your own! Here are some examples of Self love affirmations I created and use.

Self-love is kind and gentle, yet firm and accountable.

Self-love does not hurt or overpower, but heals and empowers.

Self-love is teaching the message of the Divine with like minds, sharing the word for world peace!

Self-love is good enough and deserving, doesn't have to earn or work for it. It learns to give freely, and unconditionally!

Self-love carries empathy and compassion with sincerity and compassion. Love is truth and so must be self-love!

Self-love is mindful that it's not always about you! No harm or exploitation of others to create happiness.

Self-love spends quality time to invest in the upkeep, upgrade, and evolution of self. Thus, self-improving! Self-improvement comes out of self-love!

Self-love embraces the challenge to improve, and doesn't dwell on 'what it can't do.'

Self-love is a reflection of self! So don't be a hater!

Self-love emboldens the few, to step out to inspire the many! There's only one world, and love must be in it for peace to exist!

Self-love 2 H.W.

In the Spirit of balancing uplifts: mental, physical, emotional, and positive affirmations.

Create two affirmations per uplift pillars!

Affirmations can penetrate the subconscious level. So put effort into your craft!

Last Words

You don't need to exploit anyone to be happy!

Self-love is truth and courage! Self-Love is sharing and caring!

Self-love creates unconditional love!

Self-love is what we need to save our planet cause true love lives in peace!

Self-love is embracing your cultural identity and your heritage!

Warm Ups

Clear your mind in a safe space for 4 minutes!

Then recite what you love about you for 2 minutes!

Self Love 3 The Power of Emotions!

Emotions are energy, and you must learn to channel it, so you can continue the self-work. The energy of our emotions can be very strong at times, which is why thyself must be wiser. Materials on Love of Self are immense in resources; find what works for you in a positive non-destructive way! Self-love has many layers, upon many wrinkles, and ranges that will be a part of your journey for the rest of your huemyn experience. How you manage your emotions will set the tone for your ability to self-cope!

Self-love is Self-coping, too!

Emotions are powerful energy! Why? Because emotions power the will and hearts of an individual's desired nature. Emotions, when not properly managed, can immediately change the frequency levels within us without notice! Gaining a better understanding of your emotions and how they affect your frequency is important and cannot be overemphasized!

Emotions are about a state of mind! The way of the mind is the direction its likely to follow.

Responses to events, situations, personal actions or the actions of others (directly or indirectly) can quite often cause a negative feeling or a positive one!

Emotions are unique to each individual!

Emotional energy can be positive like happy, joy, hopeful, loving, which can inspire, uplift, or motivate you!

Motional energy can be negative or unproductive like anger, sadness, fear, or anxiety, which could cause emotional pain, disrupt joy, cause stagnation in the pursuit of happiness, or even foster bad reactions!

Emotions are reactions to triggers!

Managing emotions, emotional energy that is negative can be challenging! Fear, anxiety, and sadness are a few examples.

Fear needs an escape, so write it down, let it out, and find comfort in creating a constructive response to it.

Fear of failure, for instance, can debilitating, but remind yourself that good effort and consistency is good enough!

Anxiety can cause us to become paralyzed at the moment. Know you are capable of overcoming whatever is in front of you as you have done many times before!

Anger

The energy it takes to be angry is taxing! Addressing issues head-on is healthier than holding on to a potential thunderstorm! Don't become a hoarder of negative energy. Negative energy hoarding is the dwelling on a negative feeling, emotion, or past event and allowing thyself to be re-traumatized!

Hoarding energy can also manifest to anger and other harmful, self-destructive energy!

One of the worst forms of self-destructive energy is justifiable anger. When you are certain you have been unfairly mistreated or wronged, and you mentally build a judiciary case for deserved retaliation towards another!

Healing of sadness and other forms of negativity should never be reliant on any deserved or feeling of entitled closure because there is a chance, and you may not receive it! So, what?

You can't undo the past, but you can certainly learn to let go of the energy and overcome. Find something positive, constructive to re-empower you and instill your purpose in this world.

However, if it is realistically possible to make amends, do so only if you feel safe and comfortable to do so and come with no exceptions to receive.

You should never work to get over anything, but learn to overcome it! Say, 'Self, I have more smiles than I could ever ask for coming my way because I am deserving! To prove it I will permit myself to leave it to the Divine Order. I take these memories and put them away inside a mental box, stored in the basement to forgive and move on to better memories'. Forgiveness is not about forgetting, once you recognize a trespasser against don't allow room for the same life lesson. Learn the lessons the first time around to avoid repeating the same tragedies.

You decide how you want to overcome adversity! You are not alone in spirit because like minds are sending out positive vibes until the coming of the Age of Aquarius, which is here, and huemyn suffering comes to an end!

Having and creating a safe space is a great benefit to healing. Find a space you personally identify as an area you can sit or stand to be free in good vibes.

Professional care like therapy, group counseling, or healing centers are great options if your emotions become too challenging to manage on your own! It is better to take pride in receiving help because you should, than being full of pride and prolong unnecessary suffering. Pride should never take precedence over your well-being. If you are in a destructive state of mind, you may need to seek assistance. Some traumas, unfortunately, are worse than others, which is why being open means also being open to getting professional care.

Self-love 3 H.W.

How do you handle your emotional energy in the moments of Fear, anger, anxiety, and sadness?

Last words

Huemyns are emotional beings!

Emotions are normal, using your emotions is normal because of its energy!

The energy from our emotions can be harnessed positively or negatively.

Be constructive, not destructive with your emotions!

Just like everything else, emotions can be substantial, but the process is just the process!

Motivation:

Selfless love is open, so enter a safe space to be free. Stay attuned to your calling, and you may find your selfless service or contribution to the world!

We share love to create and generate more positive vibes!

We cultivate love to produce love, so get cultivating!

Chapter 5: Selfless Service

Warm-Ups

Clear your mind in a safe space for 5 minutes!

Name 5 causes that mean enough to you that you would volunteer for!

Selfless Service

Is the ability to assist, aide, or give sincerely without expecting anything in return!

Selfless Service is also the practice of inner and outer peace. Our character enhances when we engage others in need.

Selfless doesn't mean doormat!

Giving is no different from any other form of practice! Moderation and balance are essential to avoid becoming drained or taken advantage of!

The New Golden Rule

When you are faithful and committed to self-awareness, achieving knowledge of self, and become active in self-love through the practice of loving others, unconditionally, may you then unlock your divine spiritual level!

Selfless service is a part of achieving the divine spiritual level! Actions prove lessons learned, so self-love should be conveyed through your acts of selfless service!

The wonderful thing about selfless service s there is no one way to give freely, just as long as its genuine and of great intentions.

Selfless service can build up your huemynity.

True service brings joy and blessings to you and those around you!

Examples of Selfless Service

Sharing your creative gift!

Volunteering time at a non-profit or organization

Teaching or tutoring for free

Participation in social causes!

Providing wanted and needed advice

Lending a listening ear

Donating finances or resources!

As long as there is a need and you can help then there is an opportunity to provide selfless service.

Benefits of Selfless Service?

The reciprocity of a warm smile.

You could expand your sense of huemynity and self-love!

Increase good vibes and mood for everyone involved!

Enhance your spiritual level!

Share in the happiness of others.

See the positive change you provided in real-time.

Finding and creating a network with like-minded individuals with similar causes!

Making new connections and possibly opening new doors!

Selfless Service H.W.

Altruistic giving can help heal and revitalize the soul! So, what is your selfless service?

Lastly Words

Selfless Service is giving sincerely without expecting anything in return! There are many ingenious ways that you can help, discover what you desire to give selflessly and give genuinely. Maintain a balance to keep from burning out or overdoing it! Selfless Service can elevate consciousness, which is one reason why I teach freely!

Apply the information to be the higher you, and you will find joy on your journey!

MAY PEACE AND POSITIVE VIBES GREET YOU EVERY STEP OF THE WAY! ASE'

Chapter 6: Ways to Launch Age of Aquarius

Introduction

Age of Aquarius is the new age on the horizon that will usher in a multitude of ages! The Age of Information is already upon us, as the deep state exposes its criminal enterprises that are in government, business, banking systems, etc. the world will be ready to institute a new, balance, sustainable system for all beings that will not be built on huemyn exploitation. Age of Sustainability, Age of Social Awareness, Age of Accountability, and the Era of World Peace and Positive Vibes will reign supreme and the 'Promised Land' that Dr. Martin Luther King spoke about 54 years ago is almost here.

Have your mind open so we can continue to dream for a world we can all appreciate, which is a peaceful, loving, self-expressive, and overall positive vibes world based in truth, justice, accountability, and innovative collaboration to address world issues! Positive vibes with like minds help maintain order in truth.

We need more like minds and sincere hearts, which takes a mind of a visionary! Are you a visionary? Are ready to elevate beyond what you are currently seeing and hearing? Well embrace the new and let go of the old ways that have stifled the growth of huemynity for far too long: fear and hate.

Doing your part is just becoming an ally of truth, justice, free will, and Divine Order! What you can share, give freely of yourself in a positive way is more than enough. Change happens from the inside out, so be a change agent and later you shall find the like-minds and work together for the common good. The Divine Order will not rest until liberation has been won, so wake up and become a lightworker, a healer, a giver, a teacher, or a messenger, it doesn't matter, just find your true talent and use it for the goodwill of the EARTH!

Break out of the fear and flight mentality and disconnect from any bad frequencies that don't enhance, empower, or develop you into becoming your greater self. Strive to BE your greater Self!

Warm Ups

Clear your mind in a safe space for 4 minutes

Then, stretch all the way up and take in the energy, hold for 7 seconds, and slowly bring down to your heart for 11 reps!

Ways to Launch the Age of Aquarius

We dare to break free from the old way of thinking! If history is to tell about our time in the here and now, let it be said that despite the odds, shortcomings, and insurmountable odds, we overcame tyranny and transcended to an age of truth, love, liberty, and compassion: the Age of Aquarius!

To be helpful in bringing in a new age we first must acknowledge the old age.

Food, water and air impurities. Ponzi economic system. Huemyn abuse, neglect, and rights violations!

Political corruption is full of lies and deceit. Monopoly money over huemyn lives. Prison industrial complex! Huemyn trafficking. Pedophilia epidemic. Racial discrimination and the caste system.

Current System

Child Abuse in religion, destruction of world resources and wildlife. Military industrial complex. Abuse of political power. Racial, ethnic, social and cultural oppression.

Corporate-influenced society. Abuse of surveillance and by deep state.

The list can go on and on, so many problems, and so little options in sight!

However, in chaos is opportunity. What that opportunity is and becomes is ultimately within our control.

Remember the new golden rule

When you are faithful and committed to self-awareness, achieving knowledge of self, and become active in self-love through the practice of loving others, unconditionally, may you then unlock your divine spiritual level!

Selfless service is a part of achieving the divine spiritual level! Actions prove lessons learned, so self-love should be conveyed through your acts of selfless service!

Focus on Knowledge of Self:

Being genuine in your living, be real to thySelf!

Learn your purpose and motivations!

Have a safe space to create, write, think, talk, or recharge and balance.

Know what you can and can't do; learn how much you can handle.

Embrace the combination of your zodiac and divine number; there are hidden gifts about who you are inside, so explore!

Find your balance and stay grounded. Self-love to give and share love freely!

Know who you are by staying within your abilities! Contribute to efforts through your passions and talents!

Focus on your Health:

Drink natural water and often distilled water to avoid tap water that may have fluoride and lead for instance.

Join or create a social gardening group, collective, or community!

Eliminate, if not minimize GMO food intake!

Eat more vegetables! Find a replacement for table salt and processed sugar and use more organic products.

Minimize and eliminate white sugar from your diet!

Cut out at least one fast food restaurant from your routine!

Watch out for soy lecithin in anything chocolate!

Beware of food in which chemicals are making up the majority of the food's ingredients!

- Learn to detox the body to free the mind from the toxins of GMO foods and tainted water.

Alkaline water, spring water (check source), distilled water (no longer than 2 weeks at a time)

-Take in super green foods or supplements like kelp to get some of the nutrients your body craves.

Plant a garden or join a garden club, strive to be a producer of some of your food at least.

I am confident that if we rid the body of the toxins, our minds, spirits, and frequencies will elevate naturally over time. With that being said first focus on Knowledge of Self, then your health, your social interaction, and lastly, us working as a collective of Visionaries for real change!

Check out the presentations by Dr. John Bergman and make the necessary changes you need to break the cycle of poisoning your body!

Focus On Being Socially Active:

Through every city, town, or community there is always a need for positive vibes, so share it!

Create Age of Aquarius themed art, music, clothes, plays, etc. Give encouragement and positive affirmations!

Network with like minds to create masterful positive vibes and art!

Share good in the world through volunteering. Share some positive vibes through social media to assist in breaking the fear propaganda of the mainstream.

Become an entrepreneur and create a business model that allows financial stability and community responsibility to coexist!

Be the alternative to the status quo, be a game changer on social and political issues!

Social justice needs a leader... be one!

We have so many places that need majority overhaul, but focusing on our self-discoveries and using our talents to inspire and create is the best option to avoid becoming overwhelmed!

Visionary Collective 1:

We need alternative media, politics, economic system, and civilian oversight initiatives to reel in the global corruption.

Start checking for words that might be negative or have double meanings and rename or respell words to transmute the frequency to positive.

Learn to disrupt and control how you use words because whether you realize it or not, they are being used against us!

Let's make new positive frequency words for Our future Aquarius Dictionary and design our own calendar, that's doesn't trace back to Rome or Greek indoctrinated systems.

Adopting our own Age of Aquarius calendar means dropping 'Saturday' as the sixth day of the week and fully embracing PlutDay or PluDay as the official sixth day of the week!

This day was named in honor of the recognized planet Pluto. We declare PlutDay as 'A day of Peace and Positive Vibes!' We strive to do something of good spirit on this day and every day of the week to harness and elevate the frequency of the world!

Establishing our own political opposition to corruption and the status quo is paramount to breaking the stranglehold of deceit and deception committed against the Huemyns of the world!

Pledge to be a political party for proletariat, social movement, or grassroots who supports no corporate money in elections, fair elections systems, and ethics and truth over party affiliation.

Constructing alternatives to the status quo is not easy, but it is necessary!

Visionary Collective 2:

We must create new functional economies outside of the current monetary system!

Everyone needs multiple streams of income and networks for assets to break out of the 9-5 lifestyle.

Build positive vibes support clubs for light workers to come together and enhance the frequency!

Designing local co-ops for gardening, education, and other community needs of mutual interest!

Build and fast track sustainable technology to phase out old, destructive technology and outdated practices!

Be creative where you are at and be open to collaborations with like minds to make the dream work by any means necessary! Be less of a spectator and become more interactive with positive vibes.

Age of Aquarius H.W.

Work on yourself first. Knowledge of Self is key to becoming a like-minded in spirit!

Be the Change that you want to see! Wherever there is a need or problem then there is an opportunity to create change, so be an enterprise on the go!

Find and connect with like minds who not only have faith in the cause, but are about the cause through their works! Grow the networks, grow, and create enterprises outside the status quo! We must out-program the programmers! Options are needed to break the stranglehold monopoly that currently dictates our way of life for the betterment of a few. We say, no more! Everyone deserves a place in this world. To be free, live life to fullest, and to have a sense of purpose beyond materialism; and that's what can be achieved in the Age of Aquarius!

Last words:

-These are just ideas that are only as powerful as the actions behind them!

-Contribute to your natural abilities, write, post, and create more to inspire more!

-Improve dietary lifestyle and drink natural water.

-Follow the New Golden rule!

Therefore, you have to use the provided information as a tool to assist in building and exploring who you are outside of religious beliefs without feeling exploited, judged, or pushed to follow or give anything. Do not limit your self-discovery; take chances, be open to challenges, find supportive and like-minded resources to explore beyond your comfort zone, and learn the life lessons!

Arize Visionary, Peace and Positive Vibes! Ase'

www.ingramcontent.com/pod-product-compliance
Lightning Source LLC
Chambersburg PA
CBHW070735230426
43665CB00016B/2254